KEEP ME WILD

by Raquel Franco

Raquel Franco

Keep Me Wild

Keep me wild.
Let me live a life set on fire.

Raquel Franco

Wild Heart

Naked

I stood naked before him
without ever removing my clothes.
I let him taste all of my words,
the sugar and the salt,
I left nothing unsaid.
My mind like brail,
every inch
read without a single touch.
Every portion of my identity
I laid for him to feast.
Trembling, unclothed,
I waited to see if he would eat.

The Key

He who unlocks
this brittle ribcage
will have petal limbs
and honey dipped lips.

Keep Me Wild

Keep me wild.
Don't clip my wings.
I am of the air.
I need to be free.
I'm guaranteed to fall,
face flush against the wind
and without my feathers
the earth will be my tomb.

Wildfire

Only a fool
would try to harness her,
believing the chase
could catch her.
The sound of your steps
will only cause
her embers to spread.
Your only option will be
to evacuate,
to become tinder
for her
and allow her to burn.
Fierce, is not a woman
that can be tamed.

I Will Not Wait

I will not wait
till the last minute
to come undone,
Naked and drowning,
screaming regrets.
I will not wait.
I will unravel
and be brave
enough
to bare this skin
Naked and floating,
humming; content.
I will not wait
till I'm buried
and cut open,
for them to say,
"there she is."

Wave

I am a wave, indoors
slapping against handmade walls
where pain has frozen the tides
waiting for a worthy love
to burn this house to the ground.

South

Like a thousand birds
flying south,
I will always
come home.

Hands

These hands are my wings.
We are not birds.
I am not a dragon
But these limbs,
flesh and ligaments,
work just as well.
They hold.
They carry.
They labor.
They love.
I was born with wings
in the shape of two hands.

Weak

The men that saw
the worst in me
were the ones
I didn't have the strength
enough to love.

Moment

I may be hemmed
with jagged lines.
I may carry melancholy
like a second skin.
I may require
tedious maintenance.
I may make you fall
while I stay standing
at the top of the hill.
I may leave you
with a burning house
inside your ribs.

But I will be a moment
tattooed upon your limbs.

Life Raft

I keep sailing
in this ship
full of sadness.
The life raft
sits right next to me
and I just can't
seem to grab it.

Wonderland

I am Wonderland bound.
I am.
After many, many wrong turns
and u-turns, and falls
that never seem
to have landings
I will wake to skies
of dreams come true
and lilac gardens
of curious truths,
where wildflowers, such as I,
wear crowns
and every impossible impossibility
will bid adieu.
I am Wonderland bound.
I am.
I will come unwound
and wind up anew.

Truth

More than anything,
I want promises to be kept.
I need to know
I can walk upon your words
and not fall through broken steps.

If the Sky Would Fall

I want to run wild
through a field of stars.
Take all the strength of my thighs
and sprint to feel as though I were flying.
There is no better feeling
than light on your skin
and breeze in your hair.
I just want the sky to come down
and play for a while.

Weight

She holds a city
above her spine
that no one can see.
Ankles, toes and heels
move despite the weight.
She is a woman dancing,
tears hidden behind her eyes,
iris, lids and lashes
focused on carrying on.

Float

'Neath these sad brown eyes
lives one dream left unbroken.
It keeps my core together,
stitched.

These eyes have wept lakes
under a sky without stars.
I've sworn to myself,
I will not drown.

Touch

Never let your fingers depart
from my skin. Let them take a walk
round my neck, down my spine,
between my thighs. Always be touching me,
my dear. Always.

Breakfast

He said I felt like misty mornings
and tasted of honey dew.
Breakfast was his favorite meal
and the bed, his favorite place to eat.

Wild Heart

These ribs are too fragile
to keep this heart sheltered
by merely wild feathers.

Human

I am but human, littered with salt,
an ocean with rolling waves.

Dream Catcher

You won't find me running through broken fields or
scraping my knees for some boy with fake dreams. I
have my own dreams to chase. If a man wants to fly
with me then he must have his own wings.

Pre-teen Love

I want a preteen kind of love.
Tickle my ribs till I can
no longer breath.
Pass me letters of love secretly
through fingers. Kiss me
for hours with thirst that can only be
satiated by me. Love me
like a child with wings.

Forgotten

I use to hold the lord in my pocket
tucked in the folds of my skin.
I scraped my knees upon the altar,
bled rivers of repentant tears.
But my flesh has gotten the better of me
and I've since left him on a shelf,
that sadly I only come back to
when my selfish soul needs saving.

Color Me Pretty

Color me wild.
Cleanse these dirty wings
Turn me into pretty things.

Continent

I am many continents melted into one another,
impossible to catch.
I am my own country, impenetrable.

Ripe

I think I was asleep
staring at mirrors
without ever really seeing
the girl that I was,
the girl that I am worth.
I only saw
curls too frizzy,
a gut too soft,
hips too broad,
thighs too thick.
Nothing that would truly please anyone.
I carried these heavy pictures with me
tucked deep beneath my ribs
and when someone truly loved me
I threw my perfectly framed pain at them,
furious at them for loving me,
for not understanding me,
for not truly knowing me.
They were crazy to love this woman,
this flawed, spoiled, bruised peach.
In truth I was far from rotten.
My flesh had yet to ripen,
still sour, rigid, un-giving.
So I became a caterpillar,
folded into myself
and searched for my wings
till my eyes were enlightened
and I felt everything about me that was tender,
sweet enough to eat.
I became lighter, soft and blush,
a woman, ripe to love and be loved
with no need to even look at mirrors.

Garden

She had breasts made of daisies.
Baby's breath between her lips,
blood red roses between her thighs,
a garden, he couldn't wait to swallow.

Stutter

Believe it or not,
I write better than I speak.
I bleed on paper,
stutter with my lips,
words frozen on my tongue.

Shooting Stars

I don't wish on shooting stars
for love should not be chased.
If our names are written in the stars
I'll find them in my sky.

Paradox Thrill

Tranquil grips from rugged limbs
always cause my petals to tremble
and my stems to crumble beneath me.

She was more than just wild.
She was battle scars
born with angel wings.
No one heard her howling at the moon.

Soak

The worst advice my mother ever gave was,
"Never let them see you cry."
She didn't know that my tears
would soak these pages and these
words would be my gift.
Without sharing my rain,
these petals would still be buds.

Dry Land

These clouds roll
like tumbleweeds
over this world
I call home,
a desert storm,
whipping sins
against my skin.
A spell so barren
that only my hands
can reverse the ocean
that lives inside of me.

Weeping Willow

She weeps like willow trees,
her spine curved into the ground.
She is unaware that her tears water roots,
preparing her bones to reach the clouds.

Baptism

I used to think I could find love inside
my mouth, between my thighs,
twisted in drunken nights and quick
goodbyes.
These encounters scraped my insides with
each hollow kiss,
until I awoke, hungover, my heart punctured,
pounding like a fist.
Exhaustion and solitude spoke to me,
"You can choose you.
You can cradle your own skin and wait
for one worthy to give it to."
I showered off every last fingerprint,
erased where my body'd been
and forever after when I was touched
I found pure serenity within.

Survivor

If I ever appear to be drowning,
remember...
I was born with eagle wings.

Stone

When I love I invest it all.
Every fiber, vein and thought
applies.
If I am your friend,
my love is stone.
It may hurt at times
but it is
the strongest place to stand.

Wear Me Out

Wear out my lips,
leaving them drunken and speechless.
Wear out my limbs,
leaving them tired and full.
Wear out my heart,
leaving it drumming and out of breath.
Wear me out, love. Wear me out.

Wild Animal

I've been a liar and I've been a cheat.
As much as I've changed,
my old ways still whisper secrets
into my ear.
Tempting me.
Reminding me.
I am still a wild animal.

Dirty

My heart desires to live a life that's clean.
But my flesh, oh my flesh,
craves all things laced in dirty things.

Curves

Oh the curves of a woman,
ever increasing and decreasing.
For him, rib and skin.
For them, womb and breast.
And for her, cheekbones and heart.

Wildflower

I am merely a dandelion
living against the currents
till all my seeds
run away from me.

My Mother

She poured me into the world,
flesh and water,
planted her strength
where the blood is thickest,
so when she left,
my bones were made of iron.

Tomorrow

Today my thoughts are like a hurricane
whipping into an anxious storm.
The clouds reflect the color of my shadow
and I cannot find my way out.
Times like these,
when it rains and everything is blue,
I just close my eyes to dream
and wait for morning to gift me another hue.

Melting Pot

I am but harlequin skin,
with kaleidoscope roots
that match the multiple
palettes of my heart.
I am but a melting pot.

Stupid Cupid

Cupid had it all wrong,
striking men to love me,
when the heart that needed piercing
was beating in my own chest.

Wild Eyes

The right one
will discover why
her eyes are wild.
Why she was
given
wings to fly.
Count each
and every
feather,
memorizing
her
every line.

Hope Floats

She danced within her drowning,
finding beauty in the waves
and when her lungs were nearly full,
her eyes closed and grasped onto hope
and the sea drained from her very lips.

Veteran

Her spine told stories you couldn't imagine,
vibrating from her neck to the curves of her hips,
where courage was built in the arch of her back.
Strength doesn't come without experiencing war.
She is a breathing, beating testament of a battle scar.

I am

I am not a Norma Jeane kind of girl.
Just a white tee and ripped jeans
kind of Queen.
Home is a dark and dirty bar
brimming with friends and draft beer.
I'd rather bleed ink
than paint my face
unrecognizable.
I am a dreamer.
The clouds hold a world
where there is love,
where there is hope.
I am not naïve.
I just choose to believe.

Raquel Franco

He Loves Me

He was a field of fireflies I didn't have to chase.

Anecdote

We are all born sick
but he was the vessel that carried the cure.
He scorched all my infirmities
and erased the ashes within his kiss.
He painted my soul with lilacs and lilies,
a beautiful canvas, reborn by love.

Confession

Every day he wakes to this wild hair,
pillow wrinkles and stale exhales.
We act out our morning routine
ending with goodbye kisses.
And by the tide of noon
this man will confess that he misses me.
I am surprised every time.

Crash

He shoulda looked both ways
before crossing my mind,
for I know no other way to fall
but to crash right into things.

Fire bed

These sheets
are the earth.
Our limbs, tree arms.
Your tongue
is the fuel,
the fire we make.
From touch
to touch
we keep this bed warm
long after
we are gone.

Inside Out

If you turned me inside out
skin to bones,
organs to air,
a bouquet of flowers
would sprout from my heart and lungs,
veins and stems
for you to pluck
without thorns.
For there is nothing within me
that could ever harm you.

Found

Earthly salvation I've found in you.
No longer do I roam alone.
I've been baptized in love,
a piece of life I thought I'd never own.

Marquee

You created this structure
of organs and limbs
into a cache of lights.
Your acceptance of my flaws
flipped the switch, where all
the beauty you saw within
me was placed on display.
Each passerby could see
how you illuminate me.

Fever Pitch

I roamed through the pages
of this life
in a pitch of fever
waiting for you.
Fidgeting fingers, shuffling feet,
my bones began to ache.
Then one day
the wind did shift
and you arrived
like a cool breeze.
I exhaled and my body settled
right into the arms
of all that I had been waiting for.

Home is where you hear love within the stillness.

Ambrosia

Our chemicals were fluid,
fingers for pollen,
thighs to breed.
Honey born
from our sweetest sin.

I could always find you in the deepest black,
for a love like yours glows in the dark.

Raquel Franco

My heart holds a stampede of wild horses whenever I
lie next to you.

Running Lights

I never see red lights when I am with you.
Just go,
just a blur of green stars.

Red

He was red in all his vivid love.
I could taste the crimson on his strawberry tongue.
Between our bedsheets, our hearts fermented.
He turned me into wine.

Love Is

I stared at him with round and fearful eyes.

"Will you love me when the cracks begin to reveal themselves?"

He wrapped his arms around my waist.

"Will you love me when the tricks underneath my sleeve run out?"

I folded both arms into his chest.

"Will you love me when all the beauty runs dry? Will you love me no matter what?"

He smoothed a curl behind my ear, "Baby, that's what love is." He kissed my mouth as deep as the sea, looked into my soul and whispered, "And that's what this is."

Blue

Blue is not a melancholy hue.
It is the ocean, the sky.
It is passion and wings,
a place to swim, to fly.
Blue is him.

Keep Me Wild

"Love me!"

"I love you."

And I always do. More than you know and more than the moon. You can ask me anytime because I know it to be true. I love you past the stars where there's no room for air. Between all the particles and dust my love will be there.

Fairytale

Every boy I ever met
just wanted to gaze at the cover,
touch the bind
and skip straight to the end.
But then
I met a man who opened the pages
and wanted to memorize every line.
He got inside and began to rewrite
my tale in words I never knew.

That Night

I remember that night
I left your house
with a silly tattooed grin,
shaking my head
because I knew…
I was already
falling in love
with you.
And as I began
to drive away
feeling like my heart
was headed for trouble,
you ran down the stairs
to steal just one more kiss.
That night
I left with
butterflies inside my skin.

Yellow

These stairs
have always
been gray.
Till I climbed
right into you
and everything
was yellow.

Paso Doble

Beneath these sheets
we danced
in a syncopated beat,
sweaty palms and limbs
intertwined in the rhythm
of heavy breaths.
We danced till we arrived
at morning's front door
and you finished me
on the floor.

Nameless

His smile met my eyes
and the world slowed into a waltz.
The world blurred as his hand grabbed mine.
He said hello,
my lips lit up
but were frozen from speech.
His smile intertwined with mine
and he kissed life right into me.

All this magic conjured into one moment
and I didn't even know his name.

Optimum Love

My body will always be
more than half full.
There will never
be less of you
and more of me.
If your sea
should ever run barren
my love shall harbor
all that you need.

He is more than snowflakes falling.
He is the sky from which they were born.

Warmth

We were always dancing in the flames
cause you set yourself on fire
just to ignite everything that was frozen within me.

Life Vest

If ever he should drown,
I will turn my body
into waves
to make certain
he floats into a dream.

Light

And when the rain began to pour
you grabbed my hand
to stop me from running.
You pulled my waist
and made me stay.
There beneath the dark clouds
we danced. I laughed.
You always knew how to find the light.

Raquel Franco

And with our bodies shed of clothes he put the universe
inside of me.

Morning

If I could paint our love
it'd be splattered with bright violet.

Breath on our pillow
as the sun gently sleeps.

Where the moon sprinkles sweet dreams
as we embrace between sheets.

Our love is like morning
with coffee and entangled feet.

More

"I just want you to be happy. What can I do?"
These are words I've heard spoken
from his lips again and again. And with each
time he says it I love him that much more.

Keep Me Wild

I found where the wild things are
inside his raspberry tongue.

Origami Love

Write me a letter.
Spill your love.
Wet the blank page.
Give me your heart,
folded origami love,
pressed in my palm.

Castle

It's a love that I can't describe.
I cannot find the words
that merit its worth.
You've created a home
for us,
full of happiness
created just for me,
a castle built to answer
my little girl dreams.

Chain Smoke

If I could chain smoke your love
and inhale your scent
inside my lungs,
I'd put that cigarette
right between my lips.

Home

He knew what to do.
The space between his hands
were where my cheeks belonged,
home to the perfect kiss.

Become One

I am resilient,
a woman made
with steel ribs
and willow hips.
I am more
chest to spine.
We are gold,
made to conquer,
two as one.

Full

I don't think my heart has ever felt this full.
It pours out my cheeks into rose colored strokes.
I'm grateful that the shutters to your heart were left
open.
My love sick being has floated like a breeze within you.
I hope I've filled every crevice and every beat of its
drum.
I hope you are full.

Pretty Thoughts

I wish you could hear
how pretty my thoughts become
when I feel your heartbeat,
cheek to chest.

Wild Love

Life is not whimsical nor transcendent.
It is only complicated and complex.
But with him, the world is a wild wonderland.

Before

I don't care
who borrowed your body
before me,
who rented your skin
and taught you how to behave.
You will never be the same
once I am yours
and once I am yours
you will never be another's.

Home

He is everything
familiar.
He is four walls
contained
within my skin.

Raquel Franco

Scripture

His love was scripture,
sacred,
the fluttering in my heart.

He Loves Me Not

Raquel Franco

She kept running into lost boys,
falling for Peter Pans,
wandering in Neverland,
who treat pretty girls like toys.

Purgatory

There's that place between dreaming and awake
where you're safe and you're free.
I travel from empty pillows
to the place where I'm determined you'll be.

Infected

I knew better than to take a hit
but I inhaled your sin.
You seared my lips,
branding my heart and lungs
with the letters of your name.
Cancerous love tore through my veins.
I would never be the same.

Forest Fire

At first it was so simple to forgive your transgressions.
I loved you. But time seeped poison into my heart
and trees of hatred have taken root and every leaf
carries your name. Your lies water it daily. I've fallen
on my knees begging the Lord to set you free.
Burn the forest that burdens me and leave
not a speck of dust laced with your memory.

Catalyst

My love for you... unexplainable.
It consumed me with a match
the size of a needle but I was
wrapped up in flames.
You a catalyst and I,
the only one who got burned.

I composed a symphony upon your strings
but your heart did not dance.

Intuition

"Intuition is a powerful thing," he said.

And for a split second I felt the ache I used to know so well.

"Only when you listen to it," I replied knowing that for him I closed the mouth of intuition every time.

Tornado

His soul was wild, untamable.
Not even God could catch him
and certainly not me.

Side Effects

Tears as large as puddles.
Bruises bright as lilacs.
Lonely midnight waking's.

These are the side effects
of loving you
and to this day
I'd still take all the risks.

Battered

I had a love that would've saved
me from a hurricane,
a soul on earth I could call upon.
His limbs were mine; my haven.
But he'd never let me save him.
He chose to love his solitude
dismissing my bottled up tears
and my entire battered soul
and instead of a union in love
we became battered together.

We were a tale of crying colors,
our love was blue.

Humming Bird

In a moment
I was caught
by the sight
of beating wings
in an eclipse
of emerald rings.
He hypnotized me
with his song
and then he was gone.
I was left frozen
with humming in my ear.

Damaged

You destroyed my innocence
with three whispered words
and the arch of my back.

Burning Room

At first sight I knew
we were only meant to burn.
Flammable was your touch.
Weak was my appetite.
Together we formed a catalyst of tender agony.
In the end we decided
if all these walls
go up in flames,
we might as well dance.

Starved

You were an appetite I could not satiate,
a love I could not resist.
Your wounds built barriers
I could not break
and that loved died
of starvation.

No

He asked her a hundred times.

"If I asked you to marry me would you say yes?"

The last time he asked she said no, the only answer he deserved. His fifty-foot tales and tug of war rounds all deserved, "No."

She had to admit... there were crumbs left at the pit of her heart that longed to say yes.

Walls

Your love built a barricade around my heart.
For years' no one else could get in.
Even when you created galaxies between us
my heart belonged to you.
But the distance grew too long,
the pain all consuming.
My mind built walls against you,
tore down the barricade.
For my mind knew better,
knew my heart deserved better.

Birds of A Feather

I've flown on the string of your kite too long.
Loving you clipped my wings.
We were never meant to flock together,
just birds of a feather
that couldn't be held together
and now I must let go.

Battle in the River

This water I wade is not virgin clean.
We muddied the waters long ago
with blood and skin
of a love that could've been.
With all the debris we've left behind
we still try,
dragging out this Civil War
not even knowing what we're fighting for.

Half Empty Bourbon

My glass is half empty.
Only your words are left wading.

"I love you."
"I need you."
"I miss you."

and more
swimming at the bottom of bourbon.
I sigh. I sip. I swallow.
Ice clinking, melting till I'm empty.

Graffiti

He vandalized my skin
and tattooed
beautiful harlequin letters
of a broken heart
all over these walls he built.

Chameleon

I changed color.
I painted myself from black to blue,
the tears washing away
all that was you.
Then I stood,
rising from your river of ashes
and became vicious red,
a rose,
crowned by my own thorns.

Ghost

Do you still find me in the passenger seat
smiling at you?
Do you feel my body pressed against your back
in the moonlit hour?
Can you feel me waiting to take you home
in the crowded room?
Do you miss my lips
when the radio plays our song?
Is my ghost haunting you
on all your lonely days?

Hit and Run

Traffic lights never meant a thing to you.
Red meant go and
green, go even faster.
And when your eyes met mine
all you could do
was crash into me.
At 100 miles per hour
I yielded my heart to you.
But you vanished into the fast lane
too afraid to ever slow down.

Weeping

Folded on top of a linoleum floor,
my knees scraped with tears,
I wept my heart all over
the bathroom floor. Every tear
held your lies. I screamed
till there was no more of your bullshit
left behind. I cried till my eyes,
my skin and my heart were clean.
I sobbed an ocean within
four tiny walls and swam
my way out of you.

Water Colors

Our love was water colored,
pale hues floating
on the surface of a river
that'd never make it to sea.
A canvas that I painted
by my own two hands
while yours remained clean.

Turn Back

I wish I could turn time inside out.
Go back to the beginning
where all the butterflies start.

She Loved

And she loved him with hope
shaped like corpses,
bones wrapped around her pretty mouth.
He never even knew her
till he pushed her so far
that her demons,
bent at the knees,
begged and pleaded
to be set free.

He Loved

He loved her like a whisper.
Quiet.
Almost silent to the ear
but inside his ribs
his love shook like a hurricane
so much that he could not contain it
so he let her go.

Chase

Who needs breath anyway?
With you I always found myself
trying to catch it.
Even my breath chased
after you.

Bitter Sweet

He was citrus.
Lime
and grapefruit.
Honey
and lemon.
But no matter how much
sugar I added,
we could never make lemonade.

Fallen

You were a lost cause,
like the devil with ivory wings,
a fallen angel married to his sin.

Run

Everyone witnessed you breaking me.
You calling me a whore
in the city streets before
I went home to lie with you.
They saw me crumpled beneath the moon,
grass stained knees,
snot glazed down my chin
from crying over you.
You did everything
a killer would do
without ever carrying a gun
and yet I ran to you.
I ran
and ran
and ran
and ran.
I'm glad they saw me,
for now I have the strongest thighs
and there's no more need for me to run.
I'm stronger than I ever was
and now I'm aware
the only place you belong
is underneath my heels.

Don't

If you broke her heart,
if you cut the vine,
don't tease the frayed remains.
Don't create false "Ever After's"
when your tongue waters lies.
Don't tug at it just cause it's tempting.
Let her go like you were so inclined.

Singed

His sin flamed in my skin,
singing the fibers of my veins.
It's been years since we went up in smoke
and the ashes of his wildfire still live in my pulse.

Raquel Franco

She went skinny dipping in his love,
chasing him to the ocean floor.

Hide and Seek

Playing hide and seek all his life,
he didn't want to be found,
but I did.
I loved him, flaws and scars.
Though he resisted
he cracked the window open for me.
There's no where he can hide.
I will love him
despite his walls.

Raquel Franco

Whiskey Dreams

I sip this Tennessee to forget him
knowing at the same time
when this glass is empty
my whiskey dreams will carry me
right back into his arms.

Blinding

He looked so good it hurt my eyes,
a diamond matrix burned into my skin.
But not as much as the wounds
and the aching pulse he left behind.

Raquel Franco

Infected

I've overdosed on you
more times than I can count,
injecting you into my veins
where you crawled all over my skin.
I fear if I don't sober of you
I will surely suffocate from this infected love.

Played

He always played on my mind.
Sunset to sunrise.
I thought I heard violins
but they were only fickle fiddles.
I was the one being played.

Knives

I knew he didn't love me
and when I found myself beneath him
I used my nails like knives,
down his spine
to release the pain,
a parting gift
so he'd never forget my name.

Keep Me Wild

The only thing freedom gave you was a cage flooded
with memories of my skin.

Runaway

We were a runaway love train on burning tracks.
Six hundred miles to nowhere,
two blades of grass unafraid of wildfire.

Crippled

Our love had barely learned to walk
when you broke its legs,
crippling my heart
into a fragile sleep.

Vinegar

His pillowed lips
were always dressed
in blushed sugar
until the last day we kissed
and his mouth
stung like aged vinegar.

Wolf

He led me to believe
I was the wolf.
Taking advantage
of an innocent heart.
He called me cold blooded,
never loving him the way I ought.
But he was the one covered in sheep's attire.
Razor sharp teeth behind his tongue.
A lie. A cheat.
Now I'm glad I never loved
such a deceitful beast.

Unseen

Wild vows, fragile butterflies
inside the drops of tears, I cry.

Crushed petals, yellowed letters,
memories of a shattered forever.

All these pretty, broken dreams
stay at bay as long as you remain unseen.

Flourish

I have bloomed
Into everything
you thought
I couldn't,
a wildflower,
I no longer cower
beneath the comforts
of your shadow,
a weed.
I forgot how good
the sun feels
to flourish
without you.

Raquel Franco

Lessons for the Wild Heart

Queen

She is a queen of roses,
ivory, blush,
pink and blood,
silk and petals,
velvet and leaves.
She is the queen
of everything beautiful
for she is more beautiful
than everything that is.

Burn

When the room is covered in darkness
and you're standing all alone,
sometimes lighting the match
is the only way to burn.
Find the light. No one can do it for you.
It's the only way to learn.

Not Enough

Love is not enough to keep
our limbs afloat.
Not even the ocean can avoid flooding
when the wind grasp's its throat.

Raquel Franco

Skin

Tuck yourself inside your skin
and wear it like the sunrise.
You are magnificent,
crown to heel.

Some days you just have to roll with the waves and let them take you.

Catch

Hate is catching.
Every harsh word ignites a flame,
breeds chemicals of evil through each other's veins.
Sprinkle love like water amongst the blaze.
We will all burn without love to proclaim.

Repeat After Me

What would you say to your daughter
if she came to you with blackened tears
running down her cheeks?
You'd tell her she is worthy
and more than just a flower
blooming between her thighs.
You'd tell her to never give her garden
to boys with careless hearts,
to wrap her skin in a vine of thorns
till she's greeted by a king
willing to share his throne.
Now with all these words
you've shared with her,
turn toward the woman in the mirror,
and say the same words to her.

Raquel Franco

Sheets

Disconnected is not always the result
of space and time.
Miles can exist between
the body lying right next to you.
There's nothing more detached, more isolated.
If you find yourself there,
trapped,
between space and time
it's time to change the sheets.

Carry

You cannot be destroyed,
not by man
not by woman
not even the devil himself
can turn you into dust.
Only God has the power
and he gave it to you.
Let not the weight of the world
convince you it cannot be carried.

Promises

Love yourself through accomplishment.
Always keep the promises to yourself.
For then you will always have bones to lean on.

Rise

When people cast stones
use them as your steps to rise
and never look back.

Be

There is simply no other way to be,
except
wild and free.

Crave

Your body is not an exchange for gifts.
Never sacrifice your lips, your skin, your limbs
just because he craves your sin.

Waste

Live your moments wildly
without abandon.
For once it's been lived
there is no way of going back.

Peace

If you ever find yourself
wandering without a compass
just follow your peace.
It knows the way.

Cassiopeia

You are a woman
written in constellations.
Cassiopeia, with a crown
of twinkling stars.
Take your rightful place
and let them bow before your throne.

Poetry

Sometimes there is nothing that needs to be written.
You are the poetry.
We are the words.
Mankind is the story.

Harvest

Bury the bad months
and bad days.
The freezing rain,
the hurricanes,
and the sweltering tragedies
you may have gained.
Dig a hole
in the earth
and blanket them
with dirt
Watch.
It will bloom
a brand new man
who can withstand
all the hurt.

Float

If you find them loosening the string,
Let it float.
They will either find their way back
or someone else will find you home.
Either way you will be found.

Remember

Never forget
the ones who carried you
when you were too heavy,
the ones
who let you borrower their wings
when you need more than one.

Capture

If you find yourself living just to take a picture
put the camera down.
Don't try to capture the moments.
Let them capture you.

Thankful

Be thankful.
Thank
the breeze in your lungs
the lens in your eyes
the song in your ears
the dance in your feet
the taste in your mouth
the touch in your hands
the strum of your heart
and the pulse of this life.

Ivy

Beautiful girl with the rose colored hair,
remember,
seeds have to rise through the dirt
before they can ever bathe in the sun.
Life is not easy.
I know it to be true.
But the days that shine brightest
are waiting for you.
Do not give up
as your thorns fight through the mud.
Let the roots that surround you
help you get through.
Hold on to them tight.
I promise those petals will bloom.

Rain

It will always rain.
It is inevitable.
They say the sun comes after.
But I've noticed much more.
Diamond drops appear on tree fingers.
Birds offer their voice of song.
The streets are made clean.
So the next time it rains
remember there is much more
to gain than sunshine.

Maiya

She was an exceptional young girl.
She didn't need poetry.
She was poetry.
She was born
with a fully blossomed flower
inside her soul.

Interfere

Never try to tame wild things.
They must lead themselves
toward the calm.
You will only get marred
in your pursuit to heal them.
Let them stay wild.

Bee Stings

It's gonna hurt for a little while.
But baby, these are just a bee stings.
They will heal themselves in time.
Your butterfly days are waiting for you.
You won't even remember his bite.
He won't even leave a scar.

Crowned

Your reflection wears a crown.
Even though you can't see it
and he couldn't see it.
I can. It's there
shining with diamonds
just like the ones in your eyes.

Possibility

Possibility is as vast
as the belly of the salted sea
and each day the sun bares
us the chance to take a leap.

So leap.

Raquel Franco

Dreams won't come true
if you close your eyes.

Forgive

When love knocks you down
don't give up on her.
Don't deny what God
created us to do.
Forgive Love. Forgive her
over and over. I promise
she'll return herself to you
and fill your entire soul.

Raquel Franco

A woman is not written in braille.
To touch her is not the only way to know her.

Love Equation

Her heart has been divided
more times than she can tally.
Just another number added
to a forsaken body count.
She can no longer be dissected,
for these pieces are her worth.
She deserves a love equation
where one plus one is one.

Love is a Kingdom

Love is not made of Novocain.
Affections painted on skinny bones
will only crumble the settler.
Real love is a Kingdom,
that upon entrance,
your heart should come alive
and the quills on your arms
should rise and take a bow.

Reach

Chase joy.
Choose the sun everyday
and run from those melancholy trees.
Time is like quicksand.
Do not let it go to waste.
You carry the control.
Reach your limbs
toward all that is light.

Within

No, it's not hidden between his lips.
It's not flying at the height of a kite.
It's not in the size of your canvas reflection.
It's not within the number of followers.
No, love is within you.

Keep Me Wild

Enough is all the atoms you were made of.

Prepared

Humans change like seasons do.
It doesn't take much to boil the water,
changing the tide from winter to desert storm.
Just remember to prepare for the weather.

We

It is the people that make things beautiful.
An empty carousel is just a sad, wonderful ride that
spins in the wind.
A rose is just a rose if there's no one to admire her
petals.
An empty room will always remain dark without
laughter to fill its lungs.
We, this human race, we are the beauty.

Blooming

The soil is just as beautiful as the light,
the roots and everything
that led to your petals.
We must be born into darkness
before flowers can ever unfold.

Believe

Lace your skin in love.
Care for it like a lover would.
Line your limbs with magic.
Believe in it like your heart should.

Full Moon

If you want him to give you the sun,
be prepared to give him the abounding moon.
Love cannot thrive
beneath crescent hearts.

Fire Starter

A man who sets you on fire
but has no plans to build
you a home
will only leave you
among burning walls.

Blank Canvas

What's a King
without a Queen?
A man without
his beating heart,
just a walking canvas
devoid of art.

Chasers and Starters

There are fire starters
and storm chasers
seeking nothing but
hurricane and brimstone
to infect others lives.
But only love
should be started.
Only dreams
should be chased.
Let them form
their own forecasts.

Stay Wild

History is made
by girls with the mad hair
and the crazy hearts, the girls
who aren't afraid to stay wild.

Wonderful

We are all ridiculous
but beautiful in our chaos.
Everything you are
is wonderfully made,
even the darkness.

Raquel Franco

Thank you

to the Lord for every opportunity He has given me and
every wonderful writer I have met. They have all
inspired me and enriched my life in so many ways.

to my son, for just being you. You make me stronger
and there would be no life without you.

to Alison Malee for helping me edit. I am one of your
biggest fans and I am glad to call you my friend.

to Chris Ferreiras for giving me the perfect, beautiful
"wild" girls for this project. You are ever so talented.

to everyone who purchased this book. Thank you for
letting me share my heart with you.

Raquel Franco

About the Author

Raquel Franco is a single mother residing in Columbus, Ohio where she writes poetry at the root of the human condition, love. She aims to encourage, strengthen and hopefully heal with her words. When her efforts aren't committed to the pen she is cat cuddling and listening to Beyoncé.

Find her on instagram:
https://instagram.com/raquelfranco.poet/

Made in the USA
Lexington, KY
02 May 2017